52

TIPS

...

BUILD A THRIVING DIRECT SALES BUSINESS

Becky Launder

women lead
PUBLISHING™

TABLE OF CONTENTS

A Message From the Author iii

Power Up Your Biz for Success 1

Start Strong–Launch with a Splash 13

Smart Marketing Strategies 23

Find, Love, and Serve Your Customers 37

Lead Your Dream Team 49

Additional Resources 61

About the Author 65

About Women Lead Publishing 67

TABLE OF CONTENTS

A MESSAGE FROM THE AUTHOR

Direct sales isn't easy—it is hard work. But you can step into it with more confidence and less risk knowing that you are in business with others invested in your success.

When you start a traditional business from scratch, you wear all the hats. You are the product developer, as well as the expert on distribution, fulfillment, information technology, customer service, legal, finance, marketing—you do it all.

The ease of direct sales is that you are handed a proven product and can step into an established team invested in your success. Unlike most traditional business models, you have the potential to make an impressive income with a limited investment from the get-go. This creates the perfect business opportunity for ambitious go-getters who are passionate about making a difference in the lives of their team and customers.

I have seen direct sales transform my teammates' lives; replace corporate salaries; and allow moms to reconnect with their creativity, find purpose in their work, and make lifelong friends. I'm pretty much a walking example of that. What lights me up is watching other women step into entrepreneurship with grace, grow confidence, and weave their business into their life.

As a direct sales leader and trainer, I have had the privilege of working with thousands of new direct sellers. I find myself sharing the tips I've included in this book over and over again. This is how I work my business, train my team, and share best practices with others in the industry. While this isn't a comprehensive list of everything you must know to grow your direct sales business, it will take you through the high-level journey of a direct seller—from getting started to scaling your business.

While many teach a traditional direct sales, party-plan system, you'll find a fresh new perspective on direct sales in this book. I call this persona the Modern Direct Seller. Yes, booking parties from parties is tried and true. Yes, popping up in your friend's living room to share your product works. Yes, carrying your catalog with you 24/7 is a no-brainer. As a business owner, you have the opportunity to work smarter—not harder. A Modern Direct Seller leverages email marketing and social media to reach a broader audience. A Modern Direct Seller creates her own personal brand to stand out from all the others selling the same product. A Modern Direct Seller proactively builds authentic and genuine relationships that expand beyond the living room so she isn't as reliant on party bookings. The tips and tools in this book allow you to step into the role of a Modern Direct Seller. Let's professionalize the industry and reach new customers without spamming or being rude! Can I get an amen?

You are in the right place at the right time. I believe in you and the power of the direct sales industry, and I know you can do Big Things in your business. This is the time. So let's go. This book will take you step-by-step through the direct sales journey, giving you a solid approach to build a profitable and professional direct sales business. Put your business owner hat on. Get ready to lean in and do the hard work. It's time to run your direct sales business like a boss.

Let's jump in.

POWER UP YOUR BIZ FOR SUCCESS

1

Let your passion shine

● ● ●

You likely took the plunge and joined a direct sales company because you love your product. Having a permanent discount wasn't too bad either, right? Yes, there are plenty of perks—travel incentives, cash bonuses, and unlimited income potential—but what matters most is your enthusiasm for your product. With 18.6 million people in the direct sales industry, you're only going to stand out when you have a clear passion for your product and company, and are motivated to share it with others. Don't hide it. Declare and share your passion.

Connect your 'why' with your direct sales biz

● ● ●

Taking the leap from being passionate about a product to launching a business is a big deal. Consider your "why." What is the bigger purpose, force, or motivator for you? Why are you doing your business? What are your dreams? Maybe you want to generate extra income for your family. Perhaps you're a busy mom and wanted something just for yourself. Possibly you want to sharpen your business skills. Knowing, revisiting, and reflecting on your "why" is what keeps you moving forward—even on tough days.

Become a product expert

•   •   •

You're now a business owner, and knowing your product is a requirement. Do your homework. You want to understand the features, benefits, and unique selling proposition for each product you offer. Also, learn the objections. When someone isn't interested in your product, why not? Know about other products in the market that are similar. What makes yours different? Practice your response to "Tell me about _____." You want to keep it short and simple. You know more about your product than your customers, so don't stress about knowing everything in the beginning. You will learn as you go.

4

Make a list

●   ●   ●

As a direct seller, you'll always be working to expand your network. You don't want to sell just to your mom and best friend. You need to get outside your circle. But it starts inside your warm market with personal connections. Begin writing a list of people you know. Don't prejudge. You never know who might need your product. Keep your list electronically or on paper—pretty much anywhere but in your head. A helpful acronym to jog your memory as you make your list is FRANKS: Friends, Relatives, Acquaintances, Neighbors, Kids' connections and Spouse's connections. Your work isn't done here. You'll continue to add to this list as you grow your network over time. Keep that list handy.

5

Set a goal

●　●　●

Ready to dream big? Grab your favorite pen, and journal and jot down your ninety-day, six-month and one-year goals. Identify your revenue goal, how many new people you plan to add to your team, and how many parties you want on your calendar. Don't be afraid to set the bar high with big, giant, dreamy goals. Take a look at your company's compensation plan so you're clear on bonuses and incentives. Once you know your goals, write them down and put them where you'll see them daily. Write them on your mirror. Put them on your fridge. Get a whiteboard for your office. Share your goals with your upline leader, accountability partner, spouse, or best friend who will support and cheer you on.

Determine how you want to run your direct sales business

* * *

There are many ways to build a business. Digging into your options and understanding the time and effort required are important steps in setting yourself up for success. Consider the learning curve and where you're most comfortable. Dare to step out of your comfort zone and explore new ways to sell your product. Some options include a home party, personal shopping appointment, virtual party, monthly/quarterly subscription, or vendor booth event. You can also partner with influencers or even plan charitable fundraisers. Pick one to three areas of focus to begin.

7

Own your business

● ● ●

While direct sales is often perceived as a hobby business, the income potential is real. You are a business owner, so act like one! Determine if you need a local business license. Consult with a tax professional so you know what business expenses you can write off, and make sure you set aside a portion of your income to cover taxes each year. Read through your company's policies and procedures so you know your boundaries, compensation plan, and incentives. Set office hours, and decide when you will work. The beauty of direct sales is the flexibility to set your hours of business based on when you will be most productive.

Do the training and ask questions

Your direct sales company and leaders likely provide some level of basic business training. Don't skip it. It is there to teach you what has historically made the company successful. The training takes time but is necessary for your success. Begin building a relationship with your upline sponsor and her upline. You are one of many in their downline, so don't be shy. Speak up when you need help, or encouragement, or have questions. They have walked the same path as you—and been successful. Lean on them. Seek out mentors and advice when you hit roadblocks. Go to your company conference—this is a no-brainer. Budget money to make the trip. Soak in the training, and connect with leaders in your company.

Study those who are successful

• • •

Through social media, you can easily learn from professional direct sellers within and outside your direct sales company. Follow their social media accounts to learn what books they're reading, what podcasts they listen to, how they talk about their product, and how they create their personal brand. Watch extra closely to see how they run their business, interact with and nurture their customers, admit to failures, and celebrate successes. Be intentional to connect and learn from leaders within your company. Seek out mentors outside your company to offer a well-rounded view of the industry.

10

Organize your finances and track expenses

● ● ●

Even if you don't consider yourself a numbers person, as a business owner, you have to pay attention to your finances. At the very minimum, simply track your income and expenses on a spreadsheet. Open a separate bank account for your business, and use a specific credit card to track your business expenses separately from your personal finances. This will make your life a lot easier at tax time, and you'll be able to review profitability on an ongoing basis.

START STRONG—
LAUNCH WITH
A SPLASH

11

Announce your new venture

• • •

Announcing your new business is a big deal! The very best way to share with others is in a personal conversation where you speak from your heart. Reach out in ways you normally communicate with people you know—text message, phone call, email, social media message, etc. Be clear about how they can support you—these are your friends and family, after all! Direct them to follow you on social media, invite them to a launch party, ask them if they would like to join your customer group to follow your journey. Posting on social media is a good way to supplement your personal conversations. Just keep it personal. Don't use a corporate stock photo or a copy/paste message. It needs to have your voice. Make it about you, your passion, and your why.

Establish a 'VIP group" on Facebook

• • •

Meet your customers where they are, and make it easy for them to learn more about your product and business journey. Keep business posts on your personal social media accounts at a minimum. If your customers live on social media, establish a VIP group to cultivate relationships. Don't just add people—let them opt-in to join. This group is not to sell, sell, sell. It is a place to provide value and create engagement. Be intentional about every post you write. This might include providing product tips, making your customers laugh, sharing your stories, providing exclusive deals, and having fun.

13

Name and claim your business

• • •

While your direct sales business likely has brand recognition, part of building your own business is standing out from others who sell the same product. Establishing your own business name is a great way to begin. Consider using your name as part of your business name. Keep it short and clear. Once you know your business name, purchase the domain name (URL) and claim social media channels. Be consistent across channels. This is essentially your virtual business card. Go get some actual business cards while you're at it. You're in business!

Plan a kickoff event

●　●　●

It's time to get this business launched. While we love it when customers go directly to our website and order, that's not usually the case. Most customers want to learn more about your product and need a gentle nudge before ordering. Plan at least two kickoff events: in-person and online. Just like an in-person event, set a specific time and invite your followers to join you in your VIP group. You can share content (live video, photos, and text) to introduce your new business to your online community. This is your opportunity for others to learn more about what you do. Incorporate the fun factor. Set a theme, and offer giveaways to drive attendance (even a small goody bag). Consider several kickoff events across different circles of friends. This is also great practice for you as you get started.

15

Begin to grow your customer base

● ● ●

What will make or break your business is the size of your customer base. Sure, your mom and BFF will buy your product—but you need to take it a step farther. To create a sustainable, thriving business, you need to grow your customer list every single day. Go back to the list of contacts you made. Each time you meet a new connection, add him or her to your list and track your conversations. Every day, have two conversations about your business with new contacts. Those two simple conversations add up to sixty new contacts a month, or 720 new contacts each year. Wowzers!

Ask for a sale

• • •

If you don't ask, it's already a no. While asking may put you out of your comfort zone, you must have an individual conversation with each potential customer. Keep the conversation personal. Mention that "I thought of you" or that "I didn't want you to miss out" to create a focus on the over-the-top customer service you provide. End your chat with a direct question like "Can I help you place an order?" or "Would you like to give it a try?" The more often you practice asking for a sale, the easier it will get for you.

17

Ask for bookings

● ● ●

If you are in a party-plan direct sales company, then one of the ways to expand your network is booking parties. Booking a party guarantees that you will be introduced to new customers. Your hostess will invite her friends and family, which expands your customer base and introduces you to new circles. Provide some fun incentives for scheduling a party, such as a small gift. Ask a simple question: "Did you get everything on your list, or can we pencil in a party to get you some hostess rewards?" Aim to book two more parties at every scheduled party. At that rate, your business will grow exponentially.

18

Ask if they're interested in doing what you do

● ● ●

It's never too early to begin building your team. You have an entire company and team to support your teammates' success, so don't feel like you have to know everything to add to your crew. Building a team takes practice, and it's never too early to plant seeds. Casually mention your business opportunity in conversation. Share what you love about it. Ask the question, "Have you ever thought about doing what I do?" for practice, and see what kind of responses you get. It's important not to prejudge or rule anyone out. You may be surprised at who is interested in learning more.

SMART MARKETING
STRATEGIES

19

Develop your personal brand

●　●　●

Now that you know your company's brand and stellar products, and you are building a customer base, let's shift gears and think about your personal brand. This is more than a logo and colors. This is what you want to be known for—maybe a niche within your company's products and services. Developing a personal brand is being clear about how you will stand out. Think of three to five words that define you and that you would want to come up in a conversation about you. Are you a mom? Volunteer? Entrepreneur? Wellness advocate? Your personal brand is how you show up to the world.

Build an email list

An email list takes you directly to an inbox. Rather than social media, where you don't "own" the platform and not everyone in your network can see your posts, you know with email you get directly to your recipients. Then they decide if they want to open and click on it. Email marketing can be automated and work in the background for you while you're focused on serving your customers. When you make new contacts, customers, or hostesses, add them to your email system. Delivering carefully crafted emails packed with value will differentiate you.

21

Build a website or blog

• • •

While your direct sales company likely gives you a replicated company website, consider creating your own website or blog. This gives you the flexibility to build your personal brand, provides a platform to share helpful product reviews or tips, and offers a place to express your own voice so customers get to know you better. Your website also is another avenue for your customers to find you online and for you to build your email list. In the beginning, just keep it simple and professional, and add web content as your business grows.

Invest in professional photos

Invest in professional photos at least once a year. I'm not talking a new headshot—get photos of you doing your thing. Give your followers a behind-the-scenes peek into your life. Include your family, pets, office space, your team, your favorite things, and your day-to-day lifestyle. Get dolled up, grab a few of your favorite outfits, find a photographer you love, and spend a few hours smiling until your face hurts. Your updated photos will serve you well on your website, social media channels, and marketing pieces—all contributing to building a strong personal brand.

23

Create an online presence

● ● ●

As your marketing strategy evolves, expanding your online presence will help customers find you more easily. Set up social media channels such as a Facebook business page, Google business listing, Pinterest account, YouTube channel, and Instagram account. While you do not need to be active daily on all channels, you want to show up in search engine results by posting fresh content on a regular basis. Consider these channels your virtual business card. Pick your primary place to hang out (usually it's your Facebook group), and then post to your other accounts as time allows. Your goal is to show up on the first page of Google when your customers type a combination of your name, location, and your direct sales company into their search bar.

24

Get a PO Box

• • •

As a direct seller, you're likely working from home and may not want to include your home address on your marketing materials. If you plan to include email marketing in your strategies, you are required to include your mailing address in the footer. As you mail out products or thank-you notes, having a PO Box as the return address looks professional, while also protecting your privacy.

Create marketing materials

● ● ●

Invest in marketing materials that include your personal contact information. Your company likely provides marketing materials for you to use. At a minimum, add a sticker label with your contact information to your company's materials. To step up your personal brand, develop customized marketing materials that reflect how you want to show up. Business cards and catalogs are must-haves in your marketing toolkit. Keep them in your car, bag, and office so you can easily hand one over when your direct sales business comes up. You may want to create your own thank-you notes, stationary, postcards, or notepads as well.

26

Wear branded gear

* * *

Most direct sales companies have some super-cute branded gear you can rep while you're out and about. A ball cap, sweatshirt, or water bottle with your company logo on it can be a great conversation starter for your business. Even if it doesn't become a topic of conversation, it is a subtle reminder for potential customers about what you do. Branded gear can also add a fun flair in social media posts—even when you're not talking specifically about your business.

Build real relationships

● ● ●

What separates you as a direct seller from a big-box store is that you can develop a real relationship with your customers. You can provide a level of service unparalleled by any store out there. Work that to your advantage. You are in a relationship business. While you can promote your business through many forms of media, ultimately it comes down to having real conversations, making real connections, and being authentic. There isn't a fast track for relationship-building. Know that it takes time to build trust with your customers—just like any other relationship.

Perfect your elevator speech

• • •

When someone asks what you do, how will you respond?
Can you quickly share what you do—as fast as an elevator ride?
Practice that elevator speech over and over until it flows so
naturally you don't have to think about what to say. Focus on
feeling comfortable sharing it during your next conversation
with a curious friend or contact. Incorporate your "why," and
convey your passion for your product and company. Once you
get the speech down, you'll know it. And your audience will
want to know more about what you do.

29

Participate in a vendor event

● ● ●

Vendor events are a great way to practice building your business. At a vendor event, you get experience sharing your product with others, make new contacts outside of your circle of friends, and have the potential to reach a lot of people very quickly. While sales are ultimately the goal in direct sales (duh!), consider any sales a bonus at a vendor event. At vendor events, it is best to focus on collecting leads, following up, booking parties, and improving your elevator speech as you introduce your product to new customers. Trust me—those sales will come! Make sure you have an email signup list or raffle entry form available to capture contact information.

Create a customized email address

● ● ●

While Gmail, Yahoo, and Hotmail get the job done, let's take it up a notch. Create an email address using the domain name of your business. Develop a simple email signature line, including contact information and links to your social media accounts, and add it to each email you send. Similarly, use a personalized URL to create a redirect to your company's replicated website. This is easy to set up and improves your professionalism. It also makes it easier for your customers to remember and contact you.

FIND, LOVE, AND SERVE YOUR CUSTOMERS

31

Develop a content calendar

• • •

With so many modes of communication, planning ahead to create engaging posts across all social channels can help streamline your marketing efforts. A monthly content calendar will help you stay on track. Develop a weekly theme or focus to create a more robust group of posts for your customers to follow. This couldn't be easier now that you can schedule posts on Facebook. Leverage scheduling tools such as Vizzlie or Cinchshare that have templates for virtual parties. As you grow your following on Instagram, Planoly is one option to plan and schedule your grid. Batching this work frees up your time on a day-to-day basis, so you can respond to customer comments and focus on building relationships.

Focus on income-producing activity

● ● ●

Stop perusing social media and focus on what makes money.
Gah, this is so hard—even for seasoned professionals. Discerning
what will actually bring in dollars today (or tomorrow) from
all the other things that go along with running a business (and
oftentimes are more "fun") is what will make (or break!) your
success. Reaching out to customers individually, following up on
orders, providing product recommendations, and asking for a
sale are all income-producing activities. Browsing social media,
organizing your products, or listening to a business podcast is
not income-producing. Focus on the money-making activities.

33

Provide superstar customer service

● ● ●

As a direct seller, you wear many hats. You are the customer happiness director of your business. Your customers are the heart of your business and the direct route to your paycheck. Keep them happy. Go above and beyond. Give them bonus gifts. Handwrite thank-you notes. Help with any returns or exchanges. Spoil them with giveaways. Get to know them personally. Genuinely care about their families and lives. Remember their birthdays. Appreciate them. Think about the best customer service you've received, and replicate that for your customers. When you take care of them, they will stay loyal and continue to buy from you.

Ask for referrals

● ● ●

Growing your customer base outside of your circle is critical for the longevity of your business. If you are in a party-based direct sales company, a home party or virtual party is a natural way to gain new customers through word-of-mouth referrals. You can also reach out to your customers directly to ask if they have any referrals. Consider creating a referral program where you offer a special thank-you gift or promotion (free shipping, small gift, etc.) when an existing customer sends you new business. Make it easy for customers to offer referrals; send them a few extra business cards or marketing materials to keep on hand.

35

Develop a system to track your customers

● ● ●

In the beginning, it is easy to remember who your customers are and what products they order. As you begin to scale your business, you'll need a system to help you out. Develop a customer notebook to remember important customer details, such as their contact information, order history, likes/dislikes, personal information, items on their wish list, last time you contacted them, etc. If you prefer an electronic system, consider using a tool like Trello or a more sophisticated Customer Relationship Management (CRM) system. This will help automate your follow-up process, reminding you to connect with customers at various touch points.

Make new friends

· · ·

Consistently expanding your network is a great way to build long-term sustainability in your business. There are many ways to make new contacts in your community. Join a business networking group, moms group, book club, or social club. Test out various groups until you find one that feels like a good fit for you. Join it and get involved. Show up at gatherings. Volunteer to help. Offering to be the greeter or to get involved with membership is a great way to get to know others in the group. When networking online, pick a group that resonates with you, and offer value in that group. Comment, engage, and remain visible—friendships will follow.

37

Intentionally deliver value

● ● ●

Before you post anything on social media, know your intention. Is it to educate? To entertain? To inform? Make sure you're providing value in everything you do. Show your customers how to use your product. Make their life easier with a quick tip or hack. Support their successes, and celebrate them. Go above and beyond with the value you deliver. With thousands of others offering the same set of products, you need to deliver more value than the rest to keep your customers engaged and coming back to you for their next purchase. Most important, when engaging with your customers online—be sure it is your original content, in your voice. Sure, copying/pasting a post from a teammate is faster, but it's not authentic, and it's not you! Take the extra time to make it your own.

Increase your average order and frequency

● ● ●

Time to do some math. Grab your calculator. What is your average order size? How often are your customers ordering from you? These are two levers you can pull to increase your total sales. Set a goal to increase your average order. You can easily do this by cross-selling a complementary product. You can also offer a bonus or incentive when orders reach a certain amount. Next up, take a look at how often your customers order. What if each customer ordered an average of two weeks sooner? Set a reminder in your customer file to follow up a bit sooner for a repeat order to increase the frequency and grow your revenue.

39

Bring in the fun factor

* * *

People buy their products from you because of you. They want to experience your personality, and they love it when you bring in the fun factor. Some ways to connect with customers in a fun way is to offer them little peeks into your business and your day. Be real: show the messy. Perfection is boring. Share funny memes your customers can relate to, especially when things don't go completely as planned.

40

Meet your customers where they are

* * *

In this day and age, people shop in a lot of different ways: it is so important to serve your customers based on how they like to shop. Do they shop in person or online? And if they shop online, do they prefer to go to your website and browse, or to drop a comment on social media and have you process their order? Make a note of how your customers like to communicate. Do they prefer text, phone, email, or social media? When you build relationships with customers, knowing how they are most likely to respond can help you better serve them.

41

Network and learn from others within and outside your company

• • •

As a direct seller, it is easy to simply focus on the tools and resources provided within your company and team. Look outside for inspiration as well. What is working for others in direct sales or for other small business owners? How are they working their business differently than you are? By connecting with others, you can form a mini-mastermind to learn from each other's business strategies. They're in the thick of it too. You will likely walk away from the conversation with a whole new perspective on how you can take your business to the next level. Identify whom you can connect with, and build relationships with them.

LEAD YOUR
DREAM TEAM

42

Build your leadership team

● ● ●

The beauty of direct sales is that you can substantially grow your income by building a team. Best of all, you can work with people you want to build a business with—you get to handpick them. Even if you're just starting out, you'll have support to help onboard and train new teammates. It is never too early to begin building. There is only so much personal business you can do on your own. By building a team, you can do ten times, 100 times, or even 1000 times the business you do on your own. It all begins by asking. You can't grow your team unless you ask. Imagine if someone hadn't ask you, and you never learned about the opportunity. So start asking!

Use recruiting tools

• • •

Your team and company likely have some great tools in place to help you build your team—from information sessions and testimonial videos to marketing materials. Share these tools with a potential teammate or invite him or her to have a conversation with you and a leader on your team. This also helps you learn some of the strategies in the process. Eric Worre's book, *Go Pro: 7 Steps to Becoming a Network Marketing Professional*, provides great scripting and a framework to help navigate recruiting conversations. These conversations take practice. Ask your leader to join your first few conversations so you can learn how to talk about the business opportunity.

44

Share your story

● ● ●

Your followers love to hear stories. Simply share your story and what you love about your business. Be authentic, real, and speak from your heart. This is where a canned social media post that is not in your own voice comes across as gross and spammy. Like your elevator speech, know your story about how you've grown and what this business has brought into your life. When you speak from the heart and share your story with others, you are offering them an opportunity to learn more.

45

Onboard successfully

● ● ●

Once you have a new teammate, focus on making sure she tastes success right away. Remember what it was like when you were brand-new. Some teammates are going to need more support than others. Check in with your teammates daily. As your team begins to grow exponentially, document your onboarding and training process so you do not need to re-create it each time you bring on a new teammate. Creating recorded training videos is a great way to develop a duplicable process for each new teammate who joins you.

46

Provide coaching

● ● ●

As you nurture your relationships with your customers, the same applies to your team. Develop a regular check-in schedule with your teammates—even if it's only a quick text or message. Also, build in room for regular coaching sessions. As you scale your team, coaching sessions offer a dedicated time to troubleshoot challenges. In Michael Bungay Stanier's *The Coaching Habit: Say Less, Ask More & Change the Way You Lead Forever*, he provides a toolkit for highly productive coaching sessions. Develop a regular schedule of time slots for your team to sign up for coaching sessions. Investing in their success in a 20-minute coaching call will leave your teammates feeling supported and ready to take action. Their success is your success.

47

Set the vision and culture for your team

● ● ●

As you step into leadership in direct sales, you are empowered to set the vision and culture for your team. Your teammates will be looking to you as a role model and leader. Clearly defining your vision and your big goals, and reinforcing the desired culture you're creating will set the tone as you add new teammates and your organization continues to grow. Name your team. Give it an identity. Identify your team values, and empower your newly promoted leaders to contribute to the vision.

48

Retain and keep your team engaged

● ● ●

While you want every one of your new teammates to fall deeply in love with her new direct sales business, turnover in direct sales is normal. They're not your employees. It is their choice when they want to work (or not!). As a leader, you have the opportunity to be creative about how you keep your team engaged, motivated, and working. Simple challenges, small prizes, and encouragement can keep your team growing and building. With great onboarding, coaching, and team-engagement activities, you'll reduce turnover and grow a thriving direct sales business.

49

Recognize your team's success

● ● ●

Seeking recognition is natural. Especially as a new teammate is starting her business, give a shout-out at each milestone. Cheer her on. She is working hard and deserves it. Everyone has a different form of recognition she appreciates. Consider a personal note of encouragement or a little gift via snail mail, public kudos on her social media channels, a shout-out on your team's Facebook group, or a simple text to brighten her day. As you begin promoting leaders, recognize their team accomplishments as well. Schedule time weekly to make sure recognitions don't get overlooked.

50

Find your support system

● ● ●

As you grow your team and advance into leadership, you will need a support system to cheer you on when the going gets tough. Look for leaders, colleagues within your company, friends, and family you can vent to, reach out to for a pep talk, or gain inspiration from. Not every day is easy, so you'll want a few pals on speed dial who can get you back on track. As you continue to build and grow, you will need new accountability partners who can keep pace with you and support you as you tackle new leadership challenges with a larger team.

51

'The fortune is in the follow-up.'

* * *

This comment by motivational speaker Jim Rohn is a tried and true saying in the direct sales industry. Customer follow-up is critical. But it's even more important to follow up with potential teammates. Timing is everything. Simply check in to see if they're ready to learn more. You never know what someone has going on and how much she might need your opportunity at that exact moment. Keeping on top of your follow-up will accelerate the growth of your team. Jot down notes of when to follow up with each potential team member, or mark your calendar so you don't lose sight of someone who may be interested.

52

Believe in your team

● ● ●

As a leader, you are the visionary. You set the culture of your team. You lead your new team members to success through onboarding and coaching. Set your business goals to encompass your entire team's goals. Set the bar high, and challenge your team to reach new levels. Your new team members need your encouragement, belief, and support as they step out of their comfort zone and into their new business. Your job is simply to believe in them until they learn to believe in themselves.

ADDITIONAL RESOURCES

Visit myConsultantTraining.com to find helpful tips, training, courses and resources to rock your direct sales biz. To learn more about the Modern Direct Seller, visit ModernDirectSeller.com. For checklists, video training and templates related to the tips in this book, visit myConsultantTraining.com/52.

* * *

Recommended Courses at www.myConsultantTraining.com

[NEW!] Grow Your Direct Sales Biz

If you loved this tips book and are looking to take a deeper dive into the content, this course series is for you! Grow Your Direct Sales Biz provides in-depth, actionable training for each stage of your direct sales journey. This five-part series gives you the confidence you need to successfully grow and scale your direct sales business.

Fast Track Follow Up Formula

Download eleven fill-in-the-blank emails for direct sellers. Write an email sequence to your customers one time, and reap the benefits over and over again. This proven system works in the background for you.

Launch Your Website in a Weekend

Get seven step-by-step training modules, your own website template, and exclusive access to an online community for additional support. This course allows you to create your very own website and generate leads while you sleep.

Recommended Reading:

Eric Worre—*Go Pro: 7 Steps to Becoming a Network Marketing Professional*

Michael Bungay Stanier—*The Coaching Habit: Say Less, Ask More & Change the Way You Lead Forever*

Rory Vaden—*Take the Stairs: 7 Steps to Achieving True Success*

Rachel Hollis—*Girl, Wash Your Face: Stop Believing the Lies About Who You Are so You Can Become Who You Were Meant to Be*

David Novak—*Taking People with You: The Only Way to Make Big Things Happen*

Rachel Hollis—*Girl, Stop Apologizing: A Shame-Free Plan for Embracing and Achieving Your Goals*

Gary Vaynerchuk—*Jab, Jab, Jab, Right Hook: How to Tell Your Story in a Noisy, Social World*

Donald Miller—*Building a Story Brand: Clarify Your Message So Customers Will Listen*

Simon Sinek—*Find Your Why: A Practical Guide for Discovering Purpose for You and Your Team.*

Rory Vaden—*Procrastinate on Purpose: 5 Permissions to Multiply Your Time*

ABOUT THE AUTHOR

Becky Launder is the CEO and founder of myConsultantTraining.com, a community for direct sellers looking to build their business online and offline. She and her husband, Jeremy, deliver a one-stop shop for direct sales training that works. Becky is known for modernizing the direct sales industry using online marketing to quickly grow her business. Her Modern Direct Seller framework is being adapted across companies worldwide.

She is also a leader and trainer of her own direct sales team. She's a builder, loves coaching and training her team to success, and has endless ideas. Becky brings to her role over a decade of real-world experience, and her honors include leadership awards such as Team Leader of the Year, Onboarding Success, Top Personal Sales, Highest Percentage of Team Growth, and Legacy Sales.

With a master's degree in leadership and management, she spent over a decade working in operations and marketing strategy with an amazing company that trains leaders all across the world. When Becky's direct sales business began to skyrocket, she stepped away from her 9-to-5 desk job to build a business she loves, while having the flexibility to be home with her family. With a background in training and leadership development, it was a natural next step to focus on building direct sales leaders. She is usually running from one kid activity or business meeting to the next with an iced coffee in her hand.

Learn more at myConsultantTraining.com

ABOUT WOMEN LEAD PUBLISHING

Women Lead Publishing is a hybrid publishing company dedicated to serving female authors. Our passion is to give voice, credibility and influence to authors, with a mission and purpose of expanding their thought leadership and impact through published works.

Women Taking Charge Series

The Women Taking Charge series is a short-read book designed to elevate credibility, influence, and impact for subject matter experts. The series is focused on leadership, business, the workplace, life, and money.

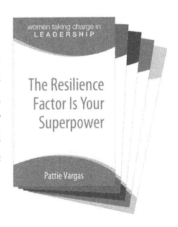

52 Tips Series

The 52 Tips series is a concise, powerful tips book designed to elevate credibility, influence, and impact for subject matter experts on a variety of subjects or themes.

If you've always dreamed of writing a book and becoming a published author, let us support you and translate your expertise, passion, thoughts, and wisdom into a published book!

Contact us to schedule a no-obligation book discovery session for *your* big book idea!

www.womenleadpublishing.com
800-591-1676

CPSIA information can be obtained
at www.ICGtesting.com
Printed in the USA
LVHW042233221019
634990LV00010BA/898/P

9 780997 601862